War Memorials

World War II Memorial

Maureen Picard Robins

ROURKE PUBLISHING

www.rourkepublishing.com

www.rourkepublishing.com

Photo credits: © Brian Meeks: Title Page; © Jim Pruitt: 5, 13, 21; © Associated Press: 7, 11, 15, 19, 29; © Wikipedia: 8, 14; © Library of Congress: 9; © Lucie Rouche: 17; © Cameron Whitman: 16; © Jim Cassatt: 22; © National Park Service: 23; © pxlar8: 24, 26; © John Long: 25; © James Rodkey: 27; © TexPhoto: 28; © Richard Gunion: 29

Editor: Kelli Hicks

Cover design by Renee Brady

Interior design by Tara Raymo

Library of Congress Cataloging-in-Publication Data

Robins, Maureen Picard.
 World War II Memorial / Maureen Picard Robins.
    p. cm. -- (War memorials)
 Includes index.
 ISBN 978-1-60694-428-8 (hardcover)
 ISBN 978-1-61590-968-1 (softcover)
 1. World War II Memorial (Washington, D.C.)--Juvenile literature. 2. World War, 1939-1945--Juvenile literature. 3. Washington (D.C.)--Buildings, structures, etc.--Juvenile literature. I. Title.
 D836.W37R63 2010
 940.54'65753--dc22

                            2009007098

Rourke Publishing
Printed in the United States of America, North Mankato, Minnesota
010311
123010LP-A

www.rourkepublishing.com - rourke@rourkepublishing.com
Post Office Box 643328 Vero Beach, Florida 32964

Table of Contents

How Do We Pay Tribute to the
   Greatest Generation?   4
World War II   6
Why a Memorial?   10
The Memorial Project Gets Going   12
The National Mall   14
Site Controversy   16
The Design   18
Tour of the Memorial   20
Timeline   30
Glossary   31
Index   32

HERE IN THE PRESENCE OF WASHINGTON AND LINCOLN, ONE THE EIGHTEENTH CENTURY FATHER AND THE OTHER THE NINETEENTH CENTURY PRESERVER OF OUR NATION, WE HONOR THOSE TWENTIETH CENTURY AMERICANS WHO TOOK UP THE STRUGGLE DURING THE SECOND WORLD WAR AND MADE THE SACRIFICES TO PERPETUATE THE GIFT OUR FOREFATHERS ENTRUSTED TO US: A NATION CONCEIVED IN LIBERTY AND JUSTICE.

Inscription on the announcement stone of the World War II Memorial

How Do We Pay Tribute to the Greatest Generation?

How do you memorialize a **generation** of people who involved themselves in every way to protect the ideals of freedom and liberty? How do you pay tribute to people known as The Greatest Generation 50 years after the war called upon them to make sacrifices? Can government agencies construct a national memorial quickly so that aging survivors of the war may enjoy its commemoration? And, where do you put it?

*Perhaps the answer to so many questions is a beautifully landscaped open-air memorial located in the heart of Washington, D.C.'s most **revered** section of the National Mall. It is nicknamed monument alley.*

5

World War II

In September, 1939, Nazi Germany invaded Poland with such force that the attack was called a blitzkrieg, or lightning war.

The balance of power in the world faced changes. Germany, Japan, and Italy, in 1940, signed an agreement to become the Axis Alliance. The agreement promised joint military action if any of the three nations went to war with the United States.

In the meantime, Britain and France partnered and became the Allies. When the United States joined the war effort, it joined on the side of the Allies.

After the blitzkrieg, the Allies declared war on Germany, a country governed by Adolf Hitler.

There was much fighting in 1940 in Europe. Hitler's Nazi Regime in Germany captured Paris, the capital of France, and tried to destroy Britain.

German troops march before an audience. Banners above fly the Nazi symbol called a swastika.

America entered World War II on December 8, 1941, one day after the Japanese attacked the U.S. Naval fleet at Pearl Harbor, Hawaii. Three days later, Germany and Italy also declared war on the United States. In the month of December, the United States became involved in military combat on two fronts. The United States battled in Europe against Germany and the Axis Alliance. In Asia, the United States was in conflict with Japan.

President Franklin Delano Roosevelt signs the Declaration of War against Japan on December 8, 1941, one day after the attacks at Pearl Harbor, Hawaii.

9

Why A Memorial?

Nearly 16 million Americans participated in the armed services during World War II. Of those who served, about 400,000 **perished**.

While there are several World War II Memorials paying tribute to these Americans, there was no national World War II Memorial in Washington, D.C.

That seemed wrong to Roger Dubin, a rural letter carrier from Berkey, Ohio. In 1986, he spoke to Congresswoman Marcy Kaptur at a local fish fry held in his town hall. He asked why there was no memorial to World War II in Washington.

Congressman Kaptur brought the idea to Congress. She found many supporters and proposed legislation in the form of a public law to **authorize** a memorial on federal land in Washington, D.C.

In 1993, President Clinton signed Public Law 103-32 permitting the American Battle Monuments Commission (ABMC) to establish a World War II Memorial.

The Memorial Project Gets Going

   To get the project started, President Bill Clinton appointed a 12-member Memorial Advisory Board (MAB). The board was to advise the American Battle Monuments Commission on selecting a site, selecting a design, and raising money for the memorial. Members represented all ages and regions of the country.

   The two groups, the ABMC and the MAB, along with the Commission of Fine Arts, the National Capital Planning Commission, the National Park Service, and the U.S. Army Corps of Engineers met to discuss potential sites in and around Washington, D.C. The ABMC and MAB selected the Constitution Gardens area of the National Mall, but through a process of public hearings, it was decided that the Rainbow Pool site would be best for the new memorial.

The American Battle Monuments Commission (ABMC), established by Congress in 1923, is an agency of the Federal government with the responsibility of making sure servicemen and women are appropriately honored. ABMC has the responsibility for designing, building, and maintaining many memorials, monuments, and cemeteries.

The Rainbow Pool area included fountains and waterworks that were in a state of disrepair. It is located near the larger Reflecting Pool. The Lincoln Memorial rests to the east and the Washington Memorial is located to the west.

13

The National Mall

Architect and engineer Pierre L'Enfant originally designed the National Mall in 1791. President George Washington commissioned L'Enfant to act as an urban planner and design the new nation's capital. L'Enfant developed the diamond-shaped 10-mile (16-kilometer) tract. This area included grand avenues and tree-lined ceremonial spaces.

Washington Monument and Lincoln Memorial

An imaginary line called the central axis connects the Washington Monument and the Lincoln Memorial, two of the most commonly known memorials. Many other important monuments are arranged and located around it.

15

Site Controversy

The Rainbow Pool site proved to be a **controversial** choice. Many people, including a group called the National Coalition to Save Our Mall, believed a memorial in the Rainbow Pool location would interrupt an unbroken view between the Washington Monument to the east and the Lincoln Memorial to the west.

The National Coalition to Save Our Mall was also concerned about the preservation of L'Enfant's vision of a park with open, ceremonial spaces. They were also very concerned about preservation of the elm trees.

Did you know?
Today the National Mall has over 2,000 American elm trees and 3,000 Japanese cherry trees.

Japanese cherry trees

Other critics voiced concerns over how quickly the approval process unfolded. In most cases, an approval process can take a long time because there are many opportunities to review the site and review designs. This was not the case with the World War II Memorial.

The Design

   Once the committee selected the site, it was time for the ABMC to find a designer of the monument itself. The panel announced a two-stage, open design competition. They received more than 400 entries. The 10-member independent design jury selected six finalists and handed these recommendations to a 12-member Evaluation Board comprised of architects and engineers.

   For the second stage, the Evaluation Board met with each of the six design teams. They chose the Rhode Island-based team led by the Austrian-born architect Friedrich St. Florian.

   St. Florian's design recognized the site itself honored not only the veterans, but the entire World War II generation. Again, the project met with controversy. Critics voiced an opinion that the architecture did not express the vision of the ABMC and MAB.

Nonetheless, the commission accepted St. Florian's idea, but requested that the size of the structures be made smaller in mass and scale so that the memorial would be more in keeping with the style of the National Mall. Moreover, guarantees were made to preserve the elm trees and to maintain uninterrupted views of both the Lincoln Memorial and Washington Monument.

Tour of the Memorial

An oval-shaped, open-air plaza, The National World War II Memorial includes two pavilions, 56 granite pillars, a commemorative area, and a restored Rainbow Pool and waterworks.

Florian preserved L'Enfant's planned, open spaces. Two-thirds of the 7.4 acre (.03 square kilometers) memorial are landscaped with park lawns. Elm trees have been restored and unhealthy trees were replaced.

The materials featured at the memorial are mostly bronze and granite. Granite was chosen for its beauty, its strength, and its ability to withstand all kinds of **inclement** weather.

Visitors can begin their tour of the memorial from any of several entrances. The memorial does not interrupt the National Mall's grand vista.

The Plaza

The memorial plaza measures larger than the size of a football field, 337 feet long (102.72 meters) and 240 feet (73.15 meters) wide. The entire oval shaped plaza slopes six feet (1.83 meters) below **grade.**

Sculptor Ray Kaskey created a series of 24 bronze **bas relief** panels also located in the plaza. These panels are set into the north and south entrance walls. The 12 panels on the north speak of events on the Atlantic front; the 12 panels on the south side illustrate the battles on the Pacific front. Most of the panels are based on historical photographs.

The Pavilions

Two 43-foot (13.11 meter) tall pavilions serve as entrance points on the north and south ends of the plaza. Four bronze columns support four American eagles each holding a victory **laurel.**

HAWAII

DISTRICT OF COLUMBIA

NEW MEXICO

Pillars

A twisted bronze rope, which symbolizes the coming together of a nation, connects 56 granite pillars measuring 17 feet (95.18 meters) tall by 3 feet (.91 meters) deep. The pillars represent each state and territory from the period. Bronze wreaths adorn each pillar which pays tribute to the fallen soldiers and adds a somber cemetery-like addition to the memorial.

Commemorative Area

During World War II, the gold star was the symbol of family sacrifice. The 4,000 sculpted gold stars pay tribute to the more than 400,000 Americans who gave their lives.

Rainbow Pool and Waterworks

The historic waterworks and fountains of the Rainbow Pool were completely restored and now create a feeling of celebration at the memorial. To enhance the glitter of the water, the vertical surfaces of the pool were lined with black granite quarried in California.

 Since the memorial's opening, in 2004, visitors have enjoyed the open-air, open-style architecture that's sturdy and graceful. St. Florian said in a radio interview that he wanted to memorialize a generation of Americans who defended American ideals and changed the course of history. What better place to honor Americas Greatest Generation than on the National Mall in full view of the Washington Monument and the Lincoln Memorial?

Did you know?

The tops of the columns are adorned with two types of wreaths. Wreaths of wheat represent the agricultural strength of the nation. Wreaths of oak represent the industrial energy of the nation.

Did you know?

Former Senator and 1996 Republican presidential nominee Robert Dole and Academy Award-winning actor Tom Hanks (pictured here) teamed up to lead the successful fund-raising campaign to build the World War II Memorial.

29

Timeline

1933	January 30	Adolf Hitler becomes Chancellor of Germany.
	March 4	Franklin Roosevelt becomes President of the United States.
1939	September	Germany invades Poland.
	September	Britain, France, Australia, and New Zealand declare war on Germany.
1940	September	Axis Pact signed by Japan, Germany, and Italy.
	November	President Roosevelt elected to a 3rd term.
1941	December 7	Japanese attack Pearl Harbor.
1942	February	President Roosevelt signs Executive Order 9066 authorizing internment of Japanese-Americans.
1944	November	Roosevelt elected to a 4th term.
	December	Battle of the Bulge: 70,000 American men are lost.
1945	April	Allies liberate Buchenwald, Germany.
	April	President Roosevelt dies; Harry Truman is sworn in.
	April	Hitler commits suicide.
	May 8	Victory Day in Europe.
	August 6	First atomic bomb dropped on Hiroshima.

Glossary

authorize (aw-thuh-RIZE): to give official permission for something to happen

bas relief (ri-LEEF): figures or details that are raised from a surface

controversial (kon-truh-VUR-shuhl): causing a lot of debate or argument

generation (jen-uh-RAY-shuhn): people born during the same time frame or time period

grade (grayd): the amount of slope

inclement (in-KLEM-ent): physically severe

laurel (LOR-uhl): an evergreen shrub with shiny, pointed leaves used by the ancient Greeks to crown victors in various contests

perish (PER-ish): to die or be destroyed

revered (ri-VEERD): respected

Index

Allies   6

American Battle Monuments
  Commission   11, 12, 18

Axis Alliance   6, 8

Clinton, President Bill   11, 12

Hitler, Adolf   6, 30

Kaptur, Marcy   10, 11

L'Enfant, Pierre   14, 16, 20

National Mall   5, 12, 14, 16,
  19, 28

Pearl Harbor   8, 30

Washington, George   14

Websites

www.pbs.org/perilousfight/home_front

www.pbs.org/childofcamp/history/eo9066.html

www.abmc.gov/home.php

About the Author

Maureen Picard Robins writes poetry and books for kids and adults. She is an assistant principal at a New York City middle school. She lives in one of the five boroughs of New York City with her husband and daughters.